A Bug Flew into My Ear!

Sandra D. Rhoads

WestBow Press books may be ordered through booksellers or by contacting:

WestBow Press
A Division of Thomas Nelson & Zondervan
1663 Liberty Drive
Bloomington, IN 47403
www.westbowpress.com
844-714-3454

ISBN: 978-1-6642-3157-3 (sc)
ISBN: 978-1-6642-3159-7 (hc)
ISBN: 978-1-6642-3158-0 (e)

Library of Congress Control Number: 2021908141

Print information available on the last page.

WestBow Press rev. date: 4/29/2021

A Bug Flew into My Ear!

A bug flew into my ear!
Oh dear! Oh dear!
Why did it go in here?
It did not watch where it was
flying, it would appear.

Will it come right out?
Oh, there's no doubt!
Or will it sit there and pout?
Will it come out if I shout?
Or will it take another route?
What would that be about?

A bug flew into my ear!
Will it go to my brain and remain?
Will it cause me some pain?
Will I have to walk with a cane?
Will I go insane?

A bug flew into my ear!
Will it make my head its new home
And decide not to roam?
Will it come out if I give it a pome?

If it stays in my ear, what
does it have to gain?
Oh no! Will this be my last refrain?
Or will it come out again?
I am starting to wane!

A bug flew into my ear!
It might stay there a year.
This is my worst fear!
Will I be able to hear?
Will it ever reappear?
I feel the end is near!
Down my face rolls a tear.

A bug flew into my ear while
I was eating plum pie.
Will it go in my eye and be like a spy?
Will it crawl, or will it fly?
Oh, my! I am upset; I cannot deny!
It will not come out no matter how hard I try.
Oh, why, oh, why? I'm starting to cry!

A bug flew into my ear!
Or was it a bee or a flea?
What it was, I did not see.

I'll go outside and get on one knee.
I'll try and try to shake it free.
Oh, why did this happen to me?
Anyone would agree.
I tried real hard to make it flee!
I ran up a mound and jumped up and down.
I fell on the ground and rolled all around.
But the bug could not be found.

A bug flew into my ear!
If it goes to my nose,
I'll smell a sweet rose and get it to depose!
Or I'll sneeze, and it will come out like a hose!
Or it might just fly out, I suppose!
Its identity I want to expose.
It's quite cold outside, so maybe it froze!
Who knows?
I'm exhausted and starting to doze.

A bug flew into my ear!
Will it go to my mouth—
Or go further down south?
Oh no, don't go to my tummy!
That would be crummy.
It would find lots of things that are yummy.
There's something there that
might taste plummy.
Whoa! My body has gone stiff as a mummy!

A bug flew into my ear!
A bug flew into my ear!
And it's such a bother.
I run yelling to my mother.
She is with my baby brother.
They are feeding each other.
Mom said, "Don't make such a pother!
We will go to Urgent Care.
There is no need to despair.
Just bow your head and say a prayer!
When you need help, the answer is clear.
God is listening and is always here."

As fast as we can, we go to the doctor.
This situation does not shock her.
She looks in my ear with a
thing called an otoscope.
To remove the creature, it's my only hope!

The doctor looked at me and smiled.
Her hands are so gentle, and her voice is mild.
She said, "It's perfectly clear.
Yes, a bug flew into your ear.
I will pull it out by its rear.
It got stuck in your earwax.
So just sit back and relax."

The doctor removes the bug
without any trouble.
It does not look scary or pubble.
I thank God and Dr. Rubble.
Then we go home on the double.

Daddy is home from work and comes near.
After a hug and a kiss, the day's
activities he wants to hear.
I won't rehash my story because
there is nothing to fear.
I simply say, "A bug flew into my ear."

Printed in the United States
by Baker & Taylor Publisher Services